E
ST   Stobbs, Joanna

        One sun, two eyes,
          and a million stars

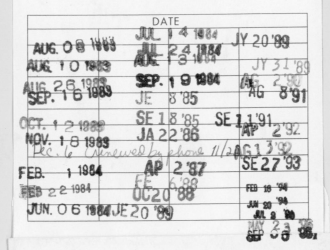

	DATE	
	JUL 1 4 1984	JY 20 '89
AUG. 0 8 1983	JUL 2 4 1984	
AUG. 1 0 1983	AUG. 1 3 1984	JY 31 '89
AUG 2 6 1983	SEP. 1 9 1984	AG 2 '90
SEP. 1 6 1983	JE 8 '85	AG 8 '91
OCT. 1 2 1983	SE 18 '85	SE 1 1 '91
NOV. 1 8 1983	JA 22 '86	AP 2 '92
Dec. 6 (renewed by phone 11/2		AG 1 3 '92
FEB. 1 1984	AP 2 '87	SE 27 '93
FEB 2 2 1984	FE 6 '88	FEB 16 '94
	OC 20 88	JUN 20 '94
JUN. 0 6 1984	JE 20 '89	JUL 2 '96
		MAY 2 3 '96
		SEP 3 0 '96

For Mirabelle

Oxford University Press, Walton Street, Oxford OX2 6DP

Oxford London Glasgow
New York Toronto Melbourne Auckland
Kuala Lumpur Singapore Hong Kong Tokyo
Delhi Bombay Calcutta Madras Karachi
Nairobi Dar es Salaam Cape Town
and associated companies in
Beirut Berlin Ibadan Mexico City Nicosia

OXFORD is a trade mark of Oxford University Press

First published 1981
Reprinted 1983
British Library Cataloguing in Publication Data

Stobbs, Joanna
One sun, two eyes, and a million stars.
1. Numeration — Pictorial works — Juvenile literature
I. Title II. Stobbs, William
513'.2'0222 QA141.3 80—41872
ISBN 0—19—279747—6

Typeset by Tradespools Ltd, Frome, Somerset
Printed in Hong Kong

Joanna and William Stobbs

One sun, two eyes, and a million stars

Oxford University Press

1
sun

2
eyes

3
butterflies

4
roses

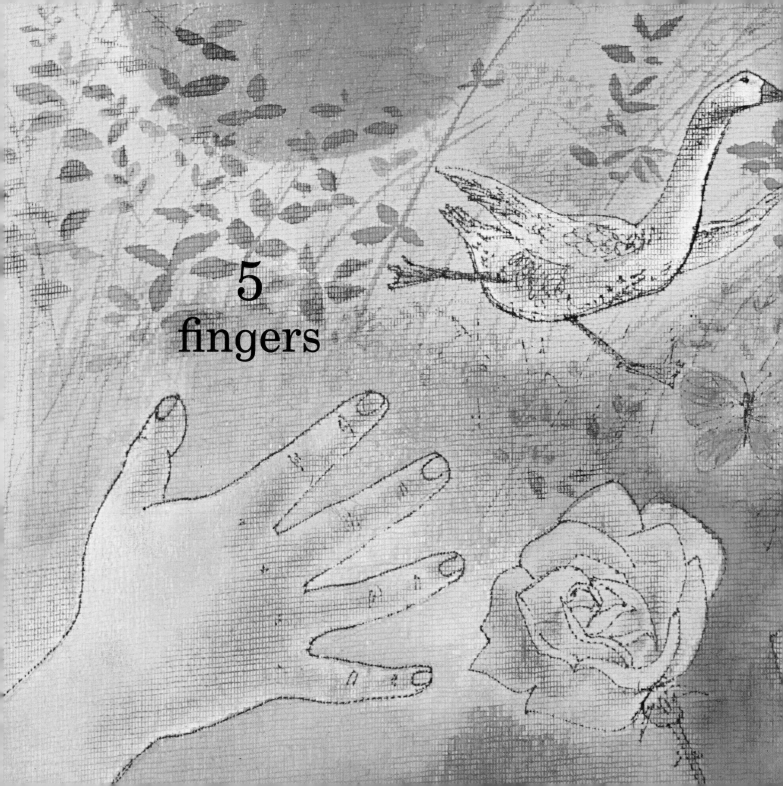

5

fingers

6
geese

7
fish

8
ducks

9
trees

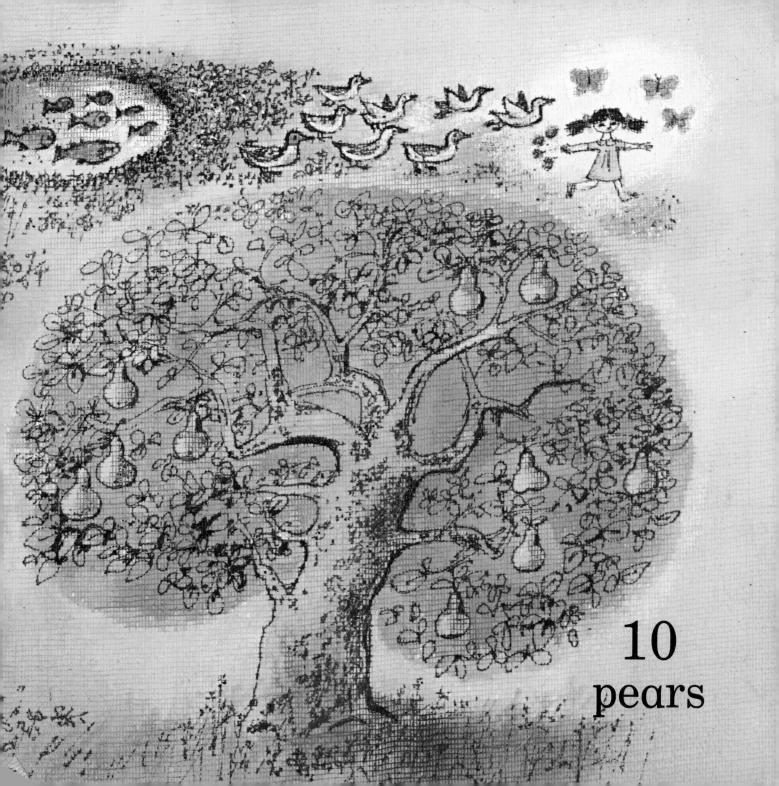

10
pears

11
baskets

12
ladders

13
rungs

14
birds

15
sheep

16
cows

17
stones

18
lights

19
steps

and a
million
stars

20
dolls